SPEED SKATING

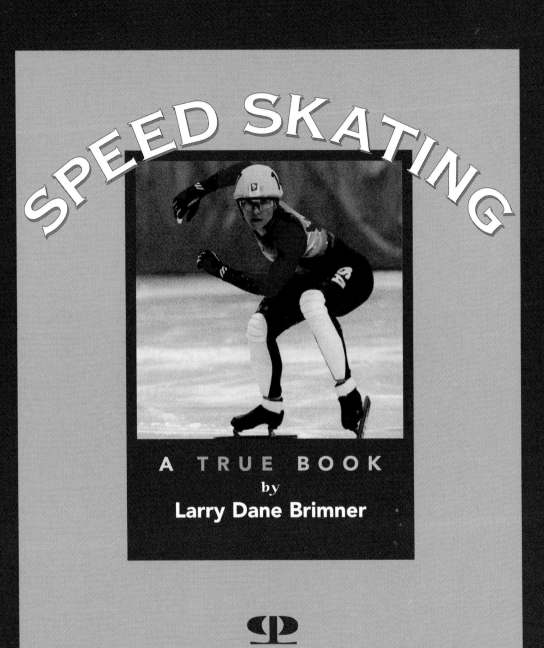

A TRUE BOOK

by

Larry Dane Brimner

Children's Press®
A Division of Grolier Publishing

New York London Hong Kong Sydney
Danbury, Connecticut

Reading Consultant
Linda Cornwell
Learning Resource Consultant
Indiana Department
of Education

For my friends at Austin
Parkway Elementary School

A speed skater
rounds a turn.

Library of Congress Cataloging-in-Publication Data

Brimner, Larry Dane.
   Speed skating / by Larry Dane Brimner.
     p.   cm. — (A true book)
   Includes bibliographical references and index.
   Summary: A brief overview of the sport of speed skating including its
history, equipment, categories of events, and memorable performances
by speed skaters at the Olympic games.
   ISBN 0-516-20451-3 (lib. bdg.)   0-516-26206-8 (pbk.)
   1. Speed skating—Juvenile literature. [1. Speed skating. 2. Ice skating.]
I. Title. II. Series.
GV850.3.B75 1997
796.91'4—dc21   97-2920
                                                    CIP
                                                     AC

Contents

The town of Lake Placid, New York (top), hosted the Winter Olympics in 1980. This view shows the speed skating oval. Eric Heiden (right) was a gold-medal winner at the Lake Placid Olympics.

Making History

Since 1924, athletes have gathered almost every four years for the Winter Olympic Games. In 1980, the Winter Olympic Games were held in Lake Placid, New York. For two weeks, skaters, skiers, and bobsledders competed to win medals. The best athletes hoped to bring home a gold medal.

Eric Heiden was an American speed skater from Madison, Wisconsin. He was entered in all five men's speed skating events. Many people believed he might win each race he skated in. Others thought he could not. No one had ever won all five speed skating events.

Eric's first race was the 500-meter event. His challenger

Eric Heiden (left) skates past a challenger.

was Yevgeny Kulikov. Kulikov was from the Soviet Union and held the world record. After the first 100 meters, Kulikov pulled ahead. Coming out of the last curve, however, Kulikov slipped slightly. When he did, Eric streaked past him and won the gold medal.

The next day, Eric won a gold medal in the 5,000-meter event. His third race was the 1,000-meter event. Again, he won a gold medal. Two days later he won the 1,500-meter event and his fourth gold medal.

On the final day of races, Eric competed in the grueling, long-distance 10,000-meter event. Would his winning streak continue? Absolutely! He broke the old world record by more than

six seconds. Another gold medal was his! Eric Heiden made Olympic history that day in 1980. He won all five men's speed skating events.

The Early Years

In earlier times, ice skating was a way for people to get around during long, cold winters. Frozen canals and rivers made excellent skateways between villages. Speeding over smooth ice, skaters could travel from place to place quickly. It was often faster to skate than to travel by land.

Skating's speed appealed to a lot of people. They formed skating clubs and began to organize races. In 1763, the world's first organized skating race was held on the Fens in England.

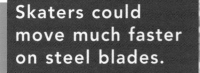

Over the next hundred years, the popularity of skating grew and grew. All-steel blades were introduced, and people realized that they could skate even faster. Speed skating races became a regular winter activity. In 1889, the Dutch held the first

The first United States speed skating team

world championship of skate racing.

In 1924, athletes gathered to compete in the first Winter Olympic Games. Speed skating was one of the athletic events. Ever since then, it has been part of the Olympic tradition.

The Equipment

Speed skates and figure skates are different from each other. This is because each type of skate is made for a different purpose. A speed skate is made for speed and racing. A figure skate is made for spinning and jumping. For this reason, a figure skate looks like a boot. A taller boot gives bet-

14

A figure skate (left) resembles a boot and has a short blade with a notched toe for sudden stopping and jumping. A speed skate (below) looks like a shoe and has a long blade.

ter ankle support during performance skating. The speed skating boot is shorter. It looks like a shoe and provides more flexibility. A speed skater doesn't need to spin or jump.

A speed skater only needs to move across the ice quickly.

The other big difference between the two skates is the skate blade. The blade of a figure skate is only slightly longer than the boot. It has a notched toe for sudden stopping. The blade of a speed skate, however, is much longer than the boot. The longer blade helps a skater to go faster. There also are no notches at the toe. A speed

Speed skaters need long blades on their skates to increase their speed.

skater doesn't expect to stop suddenly.

Speed skaters and figure skaters also dress differently on the ice. Figure skaters wear beautiful costumes. They want to attract attention and create a mood for their performance.

Figure skaters (left) wear elaborate costumes. Speed skaters (right) wear tight clothes designed for speed.

Speed skaters, however, want to skate as fast as possible. They wear thin body suits that cling to their bodies. The tight clothing helps the skater cut through the air.

The Events

Speed skating is divided into two categories: long track and short track. No matter what the distance of the race, the object is speed. Speed skaters can travel over a flat surface faster than any other athlete without mechanical help.

Long track skating takes place on a 400-meter ice oval.

Long track speed skating events take place on an enormous oval of ice.

Skaters race two at a time, and several pairs of skaters race in each event. This means that the real opponent is the clock. A racer can beat another skater in a match, but victory—and the medal— goes to the racer with the overall best time.

Long track events are based on distance. Men's events are 500, 1,000, 1,500, 5,000, and 10,000 meters in length. Women skate the

A speed skater must race the fastest time to win.

same distances, except for the 10,000-meter race. They also skate a 3,000-meter race.

Short track events became an Olympic medal sport in 1992. The races are held on a

This speed skater skates around a turn in the 400-meter oval.

In short track racing, the skaters are almost always speeding around a curve!

111.12-meter oval. The smaller oval means the athletes are almost always skating around a curve. They sometimes set their skate blades left of center because it helps them turn. Their blades are also shorter than those used in long track events.

While long track skaters race in pairs, short track skaters race in packs of four to six. There are two main short track events: the 500-meters

Short track skaters race in groups of four or six.

and the 1,000-meters. Short track athletes may also join a team and compete in a relay event. Every relay team has four members. Each racer skates a certain number of laps until another skater on their team takes over. The first team to skate 5,000 meters (for men), and 3,000 meters (for women), wins. Short track athletes aren't concerned with beating the clock. Their goal is to lead the pack!

Unlike long track competition, the winner in the short track races is the skater who finishes first.

Organized

Short track relay racing sometimes resembles a free-for-all. It is one of the most exciting events to watch at the Winter Olympics. Each team is made up of four skaters. There are *no* rules, except that the last two laps around the oval must be made by the same skater.

Chaos!

In short track relay, it is very confusing when one skater stops and another begins to race.

The South Korean team celebrates winning the short track relay.

The Falls

Certain moments stand out sadly in Olympic speed skating history. Among these moments are those that speed skaters call "The Falls."

At the 1988 Winter Olympic Games in Calgary, Canada, U.S. skater Dan Jansen was favored to win a gold medal. But only

hours before he was to compete in the 500-meter event, he received bad news. He learned his sister Jane had died of leukemia. Shortly before she died, he had promised to win a medal for her.

Dan slipped and fell during his first race at Calgary.

In the 500-meter event, Dan skated in the second pair of skaters. His start was strong. But as he rounded the first turn, his skates slipped out from under him. He crashed to the ice.

Four days later, Dan tried again in the 1,000-meter event. With one lap left, his time was the fastest of all the previous skaters. Then something went wrong. He fell again—this time in the straightaway.

For Dan Jansen, the 1988 Olympic Winter Games were ruined by "The Falls." But a real athlete doesn't quit. Jansen came back in 1994 to race at the Winter Games in Lillehammer, Norway. As the

In the 1994 Winter Olympics, Dan Jansen pursued his dream of a gold medal.

spectators looked on, history seemed to repeat itself. In the 500-meter event, Dan took a fall. Four days later, Dan skated in the last race of his career—the 1,000-meter event. This time, it was his greatest race. In record time, he zipped around the oval and crossed the finish line. Finally, a gold medal was his!

Overcome with emotion, Jansen enjoys his victory on the medal stand.

The Victors

Bonnie Blair, who started skating at the age of two, has won more Olympic medals than any other American woman. She skated so fast that some people called her "Bonnie the Blur." When she won the 1,000-meter event at the 1994 Winter Olympic Games in

Lillehammer, Norway, she also won her fifth gold medal. But Bonnie made history even before winning the

1,000-meter event. In 1988 and 1992, she had won gold medals in the 500-meter event. No athlete, male or female, had ever won three gold medals in a row for the same event. Would Bonnie be the exception?

More than sixty of the Blair Bunch—her family, friends, and supporters—were in Lillehammer to see if she could break that record. Bonnie skated in the third

Bonnie has always received strong support from her fans.

pair. At the crack of the gun, she easily skated into first place. After she raced, more pairs of skaters took to the ice. Still, she held her first-

After winning the 500-meter speed skating event for the third time, Bonnie screams with excitement.

place position. Bonnie Blair was the exception! She had won three gold medals in a row for the same event—the 500-meter speed skating race.

Great speed skaters, such as Bonnie Blair and Dan Jansen, don't compete against each other. They compete against themselves. As long as they do, old records will be broken and history will be made.

Other Lillehammer

The 1994 Winter Olympics were a showcase for several speed skating stars from around the world.

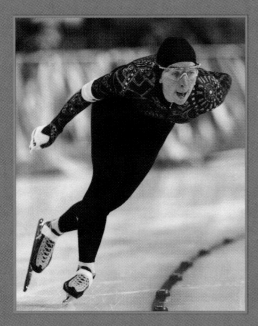

Emese Hunyady (left) was born in Austria. She won a gold medal in the 1,500 meters and a silver medal in the 3,000 meters.

Claudia Pechstein (right) comes from Germany, a country that has produced many speed skating champions. She skated to victory in the longest women's race: the 5,000 meters.

Champions

Skating in front of his countrymen, Norwegian Johann Olav Koss (right) performed brilliantly. He won three gold medals and broke three world records.

Cathy Turner (left) from the United States became a champion in the new Olympic sport of short track speed skating. She won the gold in the 500 meters.

To Find Out More

Here are some additional resources to help you learn more about skating:

Books

Brimner, Larry Dane. **Figure Skating.** Children's Press, 1997.

Brimner, Larry Dane. **The Winter Olympics.** Children's Press, 1997.

Duden, Jane. **The Olympics.** Macmillan Child Group, 1991.

Greenspan, Bud. **100 Greatest Moments in Olympic History.** General Publishing Group, 1995.

Gutman, Dan. **Ice Skating: From Axels to Zambonis®.** Viking Books, 1995.

Harris, Jack C. **The Winter Olympics.** Creative Education, Inc., 1990.

Malley, Stephen. **A Kid's Guide to the Nineteen Ninety-Four Winter Olympics.** Bantam Press,

Wallechinsky, David. **The Complete Book of the Winter Olympics.** Little, Brown & Co., 1993

Organizations and Online Sites

2002 Winter Olympic Games Home Page
www.SLC2002.org

A growing web page that provides information on the 2002 Winter Olympics in Salt Lake City.

Official 1998 Olympic Web Site
www.nagano.olympic.org

A great source of information on the events of the 1998 Winter Olympics.

An Olympic Games Primer
www.aafla.com/pubs/ olyprim.htm

An exciting site that introduces the Olympic Games.

United States International Speedskating Association
P.O. Box 16157
Rocky River, OH 44116

Winter Sports Page
http://www.wintersports. org

A central site to explore winter sports and links to other winter sports sites.

Important Words

blade the part of the skate that touches the ice

exception the one instance when events occur differently than normal

free-for-all situation in which there are no rules or order

leukemia deadly disease that results from too many white blood cells in the body

long track 400-meter oval on which long-distance speed skating events take place

notched toe the part of the skate blade that is jagged and is designed for sudden stops

relay race event in which all the members of a team race another team; one member must finish before the next person can start

short track oval 111.12 meters long on which short distance speed skating events are held

Index

Meet the Author

Larry Dane Brimner is the author of several books for Children's Press, including five True Books on the Winter Olympics. He is a member of the Authors Guild and the Society of Children's Book Writers and Illustrators. Mr. Brimner makes his home in Southern California and the Rocky Mountains.